M000200431

7 Essential Mindfulness Habits

Simple Practices to Reduce Stress and Anxiety, Find Inner Peace and Instill Calmness in Everyday Life

PUBLISHED BY: Amy White

© **Copyright 2021 - All rights reserved.**

professional before attempting any techniques outlined in this book.

By reading this document, the reader agrees that under no circumstances is the author responsible for any losses, direct or indirect, which are incurred as a result of the use of information contained within this document, including, but not limited to, — errors, omissions, or inaccuracies

Table of Contents

Introduction

Life can be incredibly hectic. You iron clothes while keeping an eye on your toddler and planning tonight's dinner. Or you commute to work, going over the day's schedule in your mind while listening to Sam Smith on your Spotify playlist.

You are always in a rush. You flit from task to task. You miss meals, rush to meet deadlines, and get stuck in traffic. It is not surprising that you are unable to connect with the present moment. You go through motions only half aware of what you are doing or how you are feeling. You don't even remember if you woke up well-rested or what you had for breakfast.

You feel that the best of life is darting by you, and you don't even have the energy or the ability to seize it. You feel restless and constantly on edge. You find it difficult to focus. You are often irritable, worried, and tense.

You yearn to be left in peace, to be alone even for just a while, and to stay still and quiet.

Scientific studies show that mindfulness is a fundamental element in reducing stress and increasing joy, composure, and serenity. An increasing number of people are turning to a mindfulness practice to help them cope with the preoccupations that prevent them from living life fully.

A mindfulness practice helps you to intentionally focus on the present moment. It enables you to be fully present in the here and now – and accept and embrace it without any judgment. It encourages you to look at your feelings, thoughts, sensations, and the details of your surroundings with an open, gentle, nurturing, and non-judgmental disposition.

Mindfulness calls for accepting what you feel and think without labeling them as "right" or "wrong." It encourages you to focus on the here and now without having to rehash the past or imagine the future.

Mindfulness Techniques

There are several mindfulness techniques that one can practice. Each technique teaches how to be fully present and engaged in the present – without judgment and distraction.

Basic mindfulness breathing

You just sit still and quiet and focus on your breath. You let your thoughts gently come and go without settling on any of them and without judging them.

Body scan

You focus on one part of the body in succession, noticing the sensations (heat, heaviness tingling, itch, etc) but not passing judgment on them.

Sensory Mindfulness

You make yourself present to the sounds, smells, sights, tastes, and touches that are present in the experience. You describe them without judging them.

Emotions

You tune in to the emotions present in the moment and acknowledge them without judgment or reactive thoughts. You recognize and label them – "I feel joy," "I feel angry," or "I feel frustrated" without judgment. You simply accept their presence and let them go.

Benefits That Come with a Regular Mindfulness Practice

Mindfulness traces its roots to the Buddhist practice of meditation. It has since joined other mainstream practices that promote focus, reduce stress, and promote calmness and inner peace.

Many studies point to the physical, mental, and emotional benefits that the regular practice of mindfulness provides.

1.   Mindfulness improves both physical and mental health.

Mindfulness relieves stress, a common cause of many physical and mental ailments. By extension, it lowers the risk of stress-related conditions like hypertension, chronic inflammation, and gastrointestinal problems. Mindfulness is also a popular intervention for problems like anxiety disorders, substance abuse, interpersonal conflicts, eating disorders, and obsessive-compulsive behavior, among others.

2.   Mindfulness promotes a healthy sense of wellbeing.

Being mindful supports a good number of attitudes that help bring about satisfaction in life. It enables you to appreciate even the small pleasures in life as they happen in the here and now. It helps you to become aware of negative emotions but not to get caught up in them. It liberates you from regrets often caused by dwelling on the past, as well as from worries that result from fretting about the future.

3.   Mindfulness helps in anger management.

It teaches you ways to become aware of the initial indications of anger and to address them in a calm, efficient, and productive manner.

4.   Mindfulness teaches kindness and compassion.

Mindfulness promotes an open, accepting, and non-judgmental disposition. It teaches you to be compassionate and kind – to yourself, as well as to other people. It helps you connect meaningfully with other people.

5.   Mindfulness prevents over-thinking.

Mindfulness teaches you to be aware of your thoughts and feelings – but not to impulsively react to them. By doing this, it helps address the following problems that arise from the stress and anxiety resulting from over-thinking.

- It boosts self-confidence.

- It promotes better sleep.

- It keeps you from feeling overburdened by daily responsibilities.

- It helps you manage a full and busy daily schedule calmly and without panic.

- It prevents fatigue caused by an overactive mind.

6.   Mindfulness   increases   focus   and concentration.

Mindfulness teaches you how to maintain focus, sustain attention, and prevent distractions from affecting concentration. It gives you the skill to remain productive in a busy, demanding, and distracting world.

7.   Mindfulness builds stronger relationships.

Being able to actively listen is a key component to the mindfulness practice. By helping you become a better listener, mindfulness helps you to communicate better and promote effective and meaningful interactions.

8.   Mindfulness helps you articulate and achieve your goals.

Mindfulness provides a sense of self-sufficiency that makes it easier for you to set and work towards meaningful goals.

It also makes things easier for you by increasing your focus and reducing stress, anxiety, distraction, and other obstacles to success.

What This Book Offers

Having a mindfulness practice is an incredible way to manage stress, foster patience, focus, and energy, instill inner peace and calm, and ultimately enjoy greater meaning and joy in life.

This book aims to help you achieve these goals by discussing broad-gauged mindfulness habits that will help you lower stress and anxiety in your life and inspire stillness, inner peace, and composure.

The chapters outline simple and practical tips and techniques to help you apply the habits in your daily life and make them work for you. Each chapter also gives an example to illustrate the application of each particular habit.

Chapter 1: Use Mindful Breathing to Let Go of Anxiety and Stress

"Feelings come and go like clouds in a windy sky. Conscious breathing is my anchor."   - Thich Nhat Hanh

Most people want to live a life free from worry, anxiety, and stress.

There is no way to make problems disappear; they are an intrinsic part of life. And they are not all bad either. They make you take an honest look at your life situation. They compel you to look for ways to resolve issues, artfully dodge certain threats, or serenely and without complaint accept what is inevitable. Everybody needs a certain amount of disquiet; it is a fundamental ingredient for healthy change.

The real issue arises when you let anxiety overwhelm you to such a degree that you lose clarity. When you allow stress and anxiety to boil over inside you, everything becomes muddled. You can't see the world – or yourself, accurately. You can't focus. You can't make well-organized plans or decisions. You become inefficient.

Anxiety also eats away at your emotional resources. You feel distraught, caught up in worrying about "what could happen." When you are not able to take control of your worrying thoughts, they make you feel depleted and drained.

Uncontrolled anxiety or chronic worrying adversely affects life. It interferes with sleep, appetite, work, and relationships. It has negative effects on health. It reduces quality of life.

Some people try to get relief from their worries by over-eating, smoking, drinking, or taking drugs. Some people who fail to find relief may become depressed and even entertain thoughts of suicide.

A Closer Look at Anxiety

What causes anxiety?

Most people think that tension and worry arise from external things.

• Will I have enough money to put food on the table?

• Will I be able to put my kids through school?

• Will I be able to find a suitable partner so that I don't grow old alone?

• Will I be able to keep my job?

• Will I be able to keep my husband?

• Will my kids be okay?

• Will I have enough money to retire on?

People worry about their health, jobs, the stock market, relationships, kids, and many other things. They worry that they won't be able to achieve goals like a stable job, a healthy bank account, a partner, "good' kids, etc.

When you look at the situation a little more closely, however, you will realize that these things are not the real cause of anxiety. How else can you explain why somebody who has less of what seems to matter most to other people can be happier or more content than one who seems more privileged in life?

Anxious feelings are not caused by the circumstances surrounding life; they are a result of worrying thoughts. They are rooted in internal circumstances.

Worry is an example of a thought-pattern.

An anxious thought or worry is a result of your mind projecting into the future and imagining things going wrong. An anxious thought, in turn, generates a negative emotion – fear.

The negative things you are imagining are not actually happening in the present moment; you are simply seeing them in your mind.

The mind is incapable of differentiating what is real from what is imagined. It reacts to what you are imagining as if they were true and happening in the now.

Even when what you fear is not yet real, you begin to act as if they were. You can't relax. You become tense. You become flustered, upset, and irritable. You are agitated, unable to concentrate, and indecisive. You are constantly on edge.

How to Mindfully Let Go of Your Worries

How do you use mindfulness to regain control of your "sanity?"

You have to be able to recognize your worries for what they are – thought patterns, plain and simple. When you are able to see them as such, they lose their hold over you.

Put a label on your worries. Recognize them as thought patterns. Instead of allowing yourself to be held captive by your fears, see yourself as "just worrying."

By putting a label on what you are doing, you become truly present. You put yourself in the here and now. You begin to realize that you have the option of letting your worries go. You CAN untangle yourself from them, and not let them take over your thoughts and feelings or influence your actions.

Don't fight your thoughts and feelings. Don't struggle with them. Simply breathe in and out deeply and look at your worries objectively. Step back from them, see them for what they are (not real, just thought patterns) untangle yourself from them, and bring your focus to the here and now.

Apply the mindfulness technique of labeling and breathing whenever you feel a worrying thought arise. Do not allow the thought to take over your mind. With constant practice, you will reduce anxiety and bring a sense of greater peace, calm, and ease in your life.

Mindful Attitudes to Dispel Anxiety and Stress

A mindfulness practice does not magically wipe out anxiety from your life. What it does is to make it easier for you to manage your worries so you can live a life characterized by inner peace and calm.

The following are attitudes that will help advance your practice of mindfulness:

•   Do not expect life to be perfect.

The present isn't guaranteed to be everything that you want it to be. It can be painful, sad, frustrating, daunting, or uncertain. It can even be all these. Some moments can be quite a struggle.

A lot of people think that when they practice mindfulness (and be in the present), they let go of the chance to escape or disengage from a present that is not positive or beautiful.

Mindfulness teaches that it is not possible for all moments to be positive or beautiful – and not all moments SHOULD have to be.

You can have a life of calmness, meaning, inner peace, and joy EVEN if your life is not perfect. You simply need to be present and to live each moment -- even the ones that seem difficult. You may even discover that you learn, grow, and find meaning the most in the moments that seem to challenge you the most.

• You are not always in control.

People who want to control everything, fix, or make everything right tend to be anxious people.

A mindful person has a better perspective. He rejoices in his accomplishments but also accepts his limitations. He does not squander his energy and time trying be perfect or to be on top of every situation.

Do the best that you can. Don't stand in judgment of yourself. This attitude makes for a happier and a more peaceful outlook.

• Be engaged in the present.

There are so many things that can distract you from being present in the present.

There are memories of past glories and successes, as well as those of disappointments and failures. There are dreams and worries for the future. There is social media, the multiple roles that you play, and the confusing muddle of things that you have to tend to.

Stop. Breathe. Focus. Just live in each moment. Give it your absolute attention. Open your heart to it fully. Use all your senses to take it all in.

When life gets too chaotic, overwhelming, and distracting for you, take five minutes to focus on your breath. This practice of "micro-meditation" helps calm you down. It sharpens your awareness of the here and now. It reinvigorates.

• Go with the flow.

Some people want everything to run according to their plans. They resist anything that is not consistent with what they want.

If you insist on having this attitude, you are likely to be unhappy and frustrated.

Life unfolds as it is meant to. Sometimes, you just have to surrender to it. To paraphrase the famous prayer, ask for the courage to change what you can change, calm acceptance of what you can't, and wisdom to distinguish the difference.

• You can't know or understand everything.

It is not a shame to NOT know everything. In fact, it is impossible to know everything.

With Google, modern man has most information at his fingertips. Because of this, he feels that he is obliged to know and understand everything.

Breathe. Do what you can. Learn what you can but accept your limits. Do not put undue pressure on yourself. If somebody asks you something, and you don't know the answer to it – so be it. That is okay.

• Trust in someone or something bigger than yourself.

The universe unfolds as it should, as it says in Desiderata. If you are meant to find your dreams, you will. If it is not in the grand scheme of things, you won't.

Do what you can and stop worrying. Stressing over things will not take you closer to your dreams. Be still.

• Re-think your goals.

If you feel that you are always in a rush, always in a hurry, and always busy, take the time to find out why. Are you driven by ambition, love for money, or the desire for recognition, success, or fame?

Look deep within yourself to find out if these are the things that you really want. Sometimes, we aspire for certain goals simply because society says we should.

• Let go of your grudges.

Disagreements, rage, grief, pain – you can't avoid these strong emotions; they are part and parcel of life as it really is. You simply have to learn how to manage them as they happen.

A grudge is a decision that you make consciously against a person. It is a decision to hold on to anger, disappointment, or pain associated with that person – even if the reason for that anger, disappointment, or pain has long been gone. You CAN decide not to hold grudges.

When you hold a grudge, you hurt not only the person you hold a grudge against. You hurt yourself. A grudge holds you in its clutches; it remains in your mind, constantly causing negative emotions. You are better off letting a grudge go and enjoying the sense of freedom from all the negativity that comes with the grudge.

Application: Doing Mindful Breathing to Ease Worry, Stress, and Anxiety

Imagine that you are in the middle of preparing for tomorrow's presentation of the marketing plans your department has come up with. The entire department will be there. Your boss will be there – and he has even invited his own boss to be there, too!

You can't stop the confused muddle of worries that fill your mind...

What if my stomach goes queasy before I even begin my presentation?

What if they notice my palms are so sweaty?

What if my mind goes blank and I forget what I am supposed to say?

What if they don't get my point?

What if somebody laughs?

What if they don't listen?

What if my boss finds what I am saying complete nonsense?

What if I don't get their support?

What if they walk out on me?

What if they think I am a failure in my job?

What if they think about firing me?

What if I can't get another job?

The thoughts run on and on and on....

Anxious thoughts feed on each other. If you don't rein them in at the start, they can build up and become debilitating. They can make you super anxious, create inner panic, and render you inefficient.

As soon as you notice yourself entertaining the first few thoughts, take a couple of deep calming breaths.

Start your mindfulness practice by accepting that you are anxious. In your mind, give a soft little nod to acknowledge all the sensations, images, and feelings that accompany your anxious thoughts.

Feel your breath. Move your attention from your worries to your breath. Follow your breath as it moves through your nostrils, through your chest, and on to your belly.

Break through the sense of stress in your body, as well as in your mind, every time you take a deep, slow breath into your belly.

Imagine the breath piercing through your restless thoughts. The breath does not force the anxiety away, rather it moves into it.

When you are anxious, your breathing goes awry. You tend to take panicky short, quick, chest-level breaths. You also feel the physical sensations associated with stress – tense muscles, clenched jaw, and fast heartbeat, among others.

Work through these sensations by taking slow and deep belly-level breaths.

As you exhale, acknowledge your worries. Don't shove them aside forcefully. Stay with the slow, even, and deliberate breathing. Imagine that you are gently nudging aside the images and sensations of anxiety with a feather.

Continue to follow the breath. Let the inhale gently move into and penetrate through the worries. Let the exhale acknowledge that you have the resources to get over what remains of your worrying thoughts.

Refrain from controlling or forcing. Simply let awareness move into and around the images, sensations, and thoughts.

Chapter 2: Dealing with Anger: Quench the Fire Before It Gets Out of Hand

"Anger is like a howling baby, suffering and crying. The baby needs his mother to embrace him. You are the mother for your baby, your anger. The moment you begin to practice breathing mindfully in and out, you have the energy of a mother, to cradle and embrace the baby. Just embracing your anger, just breathing in and breathing out, that is good enough. The baby will feel relief right away."

"Just by breathing deeply on your anger, you will calm it. You are being mindful of your anger, not suppressing it...touching it with the energy of mindfulness."

- Thich Nhat Hanh

Anger is a natural emotion. When someone treats you unjustly, talks to you without respect, or behaves in a dreadful manner towards you, you are bound to feel angry.

Anger, however, can get out of hand. If you are not able to control your anger and, instead, allow it to control you, the emotion can cause you to say harsh, hurting things, behave irrationally, and do both yourself and the other person harm.

Opt to use mindfulness to effectively cope with your anger before it escalates and becomes difficult to quench.

A Mindful View of Anger

Anger is a strong emotion. When you let it explode, it can be a source of guilt, remorse, and shame.

When you use the lens of mindfulness to understand what anger is, you will realize the following essential points:

Anger is plain energy. It is not good; it is not bad. It can lead to problems when you engage with it with the following behaviors – identifying with it, holding on to it, and letting it consume you.

Just like other strong emotions, anger provokes you to act out, either through action or words, and give vent to it. When someone does something that strongly upsets you, you tend to stew on it. Your intense angry thoughts tend to stoke the fire of your anger. Unless you decide to step back and disengage yourself from the intensity of your feelings, they are likely to erupt.

Mindfulness gives you the tool to work through your anger in calm, measured, and skillful ways.

Choose not to let anger provoke unproductive behaviors. Seek to acknowledge the emotion and to accept, understand, and calm it – and not allow it to spiral out of control.

Mindfulness lets you transform your volatile, reactive mindset into a calmer, well-considered, and more helpful outlook.

It helps you to recognize the point when the flame of anger begins. It allows you to see the emotion clearly – but without getting involved in it. It helps you acknowledge the presence of the emotion, accept it, and see it as nothing but fleeting energy. It helps you see it with clarity and objectivity and to channel and express it in more appropriate and productive ways.

Strengthening the Mindfulness Practice for Managing Anger

The following steps can help put you in a stronger and more mindful position to douse the fires of anger:

• Avoid seeing things as either black or white.

Over-generalization tends to fuel anger.

You tend to get angry when you look at a problem and see it as more important or bigger than it actually is. You over-generalize by using words like "everybody," "nobody," "always,", or "never."

Over-generalization makes you exaggerate a situation. It provokes you to become angry – sometimes without due cause.

"You never pay attention to what I say."

"You are always disrespectful towards me."

"You always do things that make people think badly of me."

"Nobody seems to care about anything that happens here."

"We are never on time for anything because you don't care a bit about getting ready; you always wait for me to remind you."

"Everybody expects me to do everything for them."

The mindful solution to over-generalization is to be conscious of the fact that the situation may be an exception. Be specific and accurate when looking at situations. Instead of thinking that "He is never on time," be exact with your observation. "This is the 2nd time this month that he is late." Looking at a situation accurately prevents you from having unwarranted feelings of frustration and anger.

- Use coping thoughts when viewing situations.

The following coping thoughts help to ground you and stop the flames of your anger.

"I don't have to get upset or be angry. I just have to get the facts right and I will be okay."

"I want to evaluate the situation accurately. How often does he really do this?"

"I don't want to generalize; it just makes things look worse. I simply need to relax and the situation will calm down."

When things go wrong, make the conscious effort not to over-generalize or look at things as black or white. This will help you stem your anger.

- Avoid mind-reading.

Do not assume that you know exactly how the other person feels or what he is thinking. "So you think I am a nagger, don't you?" "You are ignoring what I say to show rebellion, aren't you?" Assuming things and thinking that you can read minds sets you up to feel angry even when there is no reason to.

- Do not "collect straws."

People who do this as a matter of habit tend to overlook what is going right in their lives. They tend to ignore anything positive. Instead, they focus on small irritations, things which are often relatively minor, and build these up until the "final straw" leads them to explode.

- Do not blame others for your anger.

Own your emotions; take responsibility for them. "He always makes me angry." "He is always at fault." It is not always somebody else's fault when things do not go right in your world.

- Dissipate frustration or anger through mindful physical exertion.

A person who is anxious or stressed out is easily provoked into getting angry.

Reduce anxiety by looking for a productive outlet for pent-up emotions and energy. Look for a sport or form of exercise that you enjoy doing and do that regularly. Studies show that when you exercise regularly you help build your resilience to anxiety or stress.

- Be aware of things around you; use your senses.

Enjoy music mindfully. Listen to the chirping of the birds. Take in the beautiful blue sky. Feel the touch of the refreshing breeze against your skin. Enjoy the scent of your favorite calming bath salts. Savor a piece of really good dark chocolate.

Application: Mindfully Coping with Your Anger

When you find yourself about to explode in anger, take time off. Cope with your anger by taking the following steps:

- Take note of what you feel physically when you become angry.

Anger is usually accompanied by certain physical sensations. Take stock of the sensations that you feel in your body.

Your blood rushes to the head.

Your face turns hot and red.

Your chest is tight and heavy.

Your shoulders are tense.

Your heart beat speeds up.

Your muscles feel tight.

Your jaw becomes taut.

You grit your teeth.

You clench your fists.

You feel sick in your stomach.

Your heart beats rapidly.

You find it difficult to breath.

Become aware of these sensations. Pay attention to them.

- Take note of what you are thinking or feeling.

Are you thinking that life is not fair? Or that the other person is unjust or unreasonable? Do you want to scream, or cry, or run away? Do you feel like hitting somebody? Do you feel like hurting the other person or even yourself?

- Do mindful breathing.

Use your breath to address the physical sensations. Closing your eyes may help you focus on your breathing.

Take long, slow, and deep breaths. Imagine the air as it enters your nose, goes through your chest, and fills out your belly. Imagine each breath helping you relax your taut shoulders, clenched fists, uptight stomach, and rigid muscles.

Breathe out slowly. Imagine the breath going up from your belly, through to your chest, and out of your nose, taking with it the tension that your body feels because of your anger. Imagine each breath reduce the negative feelings that come with being angry.

- Think about where your anger can take you.

Look at the present situation. Think about how anger can start from a seemingly simple burning sensation and how (if you allow it to) it can turn into a raging fire that can be quite difficult to douse.

Reflect about how your breathing helps to cool down the flame of anger that is within you.

- Step back.

Try to disengage yourself from what you are going through.

See yourself as actively observing the sensations, thoughts, and feelings that come with the anger. Dissociate yourself from these emotions. You are observing these emotions; they are not you.

- Open yourself to positive feelings.

Try to replace your angry feelings with a sense of calmness, understanding, and kindness. Stay with these positive feelings as best you can.

- Communicate.

Talk to the other person only when you feel that the strength of your anger has dissolved – not before then. Express your thoughts and feelings in a constructive manner. Do not make accusations. Instead, use "I" statements to let the other person realize how his behavior is affecting you.

While you are trying to communicate with the other person, remain in touch with your own feelings, letting go of any aggression that may arise. You want to be honest and open in a way that leads to a fruitful conversation and a productive end result.

It is not easy to cope with anger. You have to acknowledge this to yourself. By taking these steps every single time that you feel the fire of anger start to rage within you, you have a better chance at cooling the flames. With continuing mindful practice of dousing the flames of anger before they can become a raging, uncontrollable fire, you will become more adept at it.

Chapter 3: Mindfulness and Love: Listen with Your Heart

"It is only with the heart that one can see rightly. What is essential is invisible to the eye." – Antoine de Saint-Exupéry, The Little Prince

"Be kind whenever possible. It is always possible." ~Dalai Lama

No one should take love (self-love, romantic love, love for family and friends) for granted.

Love does not grow on its own. It needs to be nourished, fostered, and cherished if it is to grow and flourish.

Love begins by being fully present to the other person. It begins with opening your heart by actively listening to (as compared to just hearing) what the other person is saying. When you sense that someone finds you important enough to focus his attention and energy on you, you get a sweet, gratifying, and affirming feeling that you matter, really matter, to that person. And this feeling often inspires you to show someone else that same attention.

You can't force other people to mindfully listen to you. What you CAN do is to develop your own mindful listening skills, affirm people, especially those that you love, and probably inspire others to do the same thing.

Be attentive to the other person. Be present. Stay open, accepting, and unbiased. Receive what he is saying – even if you don't agree with his ideas. Accept that what he is saying is shaped by his unique experiences, needs, feelings, and views.

Connecting with people you love in this way leads to a recognition and acceptance of each other's uniqueness, kindness, and compassion. It also makes the other person feel accepted and loved – and develops in him a bias for returning the same quality of attention and love that he is getting.

Tips for Developing a Mindful Connection with People You Love

Here are some ways that you can connect with those you love in a mindful, authentic, and loving way.

• Really see the other person.

Make genuine eye contact. This activates a deep sense of connection. The intimacy of this simple act can make you feel vulnerable at first, but it softens your heart and activates feelings of warmth and openness.

• Listen intently.

Do not just hear what the other person is saying. Listen to him actively. This means tuning in to him fully. What is he saying with his posture and body language? What is the tone of his voice telling you? What is the real message behind his words?

It also means putting aside your own ideas and feelings while you listen to him. You don't want to compromise your focus by shifting your attention to planning what you will say in response.

- Know the value of touch.

Human touch is a fundamental ingredient to one's sense of well-being. Studies show that it is one of the critical psychological/emotional resources for development.

Touch indicates connectedness. It soothes and makes you feel safe. It conveys care and concern. It indicates love and compassion.

Reach out to your loved ones by giving them a gentle and loving pat on the arm or shoulder. Doing this on a regular basis will help open hearts. It leads to a deeper sense of connection.

- Give mindful hugs.

A good hug makes a person feel good. It affirms him. Studies even show that being hugged on a regular basis helps to lower blood pressure, soothe and relax, ease stress, and release oxytocin (also called the "love hormone".)

- Do not take the person you love for granted.

Curiosity and an open mind are essential to mindfulness. They help fight complacence, smugness, and the loss of wonder in relationships.

When your mind tells you that you know a person so well that he becomes predictable to you, you tend to lose some of the wonder and magic which should be part of all good relationships.

Try to sustain your interest in the person that you love. Be open to him as if you were just getting to know him. Look for something new to unveil about him. This mindful attitude will help to foster warmth and deepen the bonds of friendship and love.

- Carve out time for the people important to you.

People often take those that they love for granted. It seems easier to break commitments that you make to family and friends than those that you make with people you work with or do business with.

Identify the people who energize, nourish, and love you. Give them the time that they deserve. Be present to them. Appreciation, respect, trust, and connectedness flourish only when you take the time to be in the here and now with the people who matter to you.

- Get to know yourself.

To be a good listener to other people, you need to be a good listener to yourself. When you have self-awareness

– you know your needs, beliefs, fears, and opinions, you have the inner space to mindfully listen to others.

• Communicate your feelings and needs.

Just as you make the time and effort to get to know the other person, help him understand you better also. Be open. Build trust. Communicate what you think, feel, and need.

One other upside to this willingness to reveal your thoughts, needs, and feelings to the other person is that it calls for you to look deep down into yourself. You need to identify what you want to share, to gain clarity, and to grow in self-understanding.

• Be mindful about what you say.

It is not unusual for a person to say something and then later deeply regret doing so. Resist the urge to blurt out everything that comes to your mind.

Is what you are going to say true? Is it necessary? Will it be helpful for the other person to know it? Are you the best person to tell him? Is it kind?

If you find yourself in the middle of a raw and hurtful confrontation with another person, you can still stem the flow of hurting words. When you notice that you are over-reacting or getting angry, choose to step back and take time-out. Opt to remain silent and to use the time to take deep breaths.

- Be kind.

A kind person draws people to him like a magnet. Practice kindness all the time. It makes people feel good; it makes YOU feel good. Kindness multiplies the opportunities to open hearts, make positive connections, bring joy, and improve health, well-being, and outlook all around.

- Practice compassion.

People are different from one another. Each one is unique.

If you look at it from a different point of view, however, most people are really just like you – they need to feel that they belong. They need to feel that someone understands them. They need to feel that someone cares for them and loves them.

When you are struck by how different a person's views are from you, step back a bit and dwell on how he is "just like me." This will foster a sense of warmth and compassion towards that person.

- Feel for others when they experience joy in their lives.

Pay attention to the good that is happening in other people's lives. Be happy for them.

Sometimes, this joy for other people's good fortune arises naturally. Sometimes, you have to intentionally cultivate it. Telling somebody that you are happy for them or congratulating them on a job well done results in positive feelings all around. It also builds or strengthens connections.

- Apply mindfulness and have "healthy" arguments.

Even healthy, happy relationships go through difficult times. A discussion can spring up, cause friction, and leave you dazed, hurting, and lost. When you get hurt, you become defensive or wary. Feeling this way can block the growth of relationships.

Is it possible to engage in "mindful" fights or "healthy" arguments? It is. Arguing or fighting mindfully may initially sound like a tall order, but you can do it if you are willing to do so with an open heart.

What are the components of a mindful fight or a healthy argument?

Breathe.

Breath is a fundamental element in meditation. It acts as a pause button. Breath also serves the same purpose in a mindful fight.

When a loved one says something or behaves in a manner that triggers a surprisingly strong emotion in you, do NOT react.

Instead, take a deep breath, step back, and try to focus on the sensations that are going on inside you. Is your face flushed from anger? Are your fists clenched from trying to control your temper? Is your chest heaving from frustration? Simply observe what is going on inside you. Do not react.

Center

Mindful breathing enables you to become present in your body, to be in the here and now, to be centered. By being present and centered, you are better able to listen to your feelings. You also put yourself in a better position to listen to the other person and consider his feelings.

Connect

When you are centered and present, you become curious, less judgmental, and less reactive. You are able to communicate how you feel without feeling the need to blame or to act adversely. You are able to respond in a more cordial, heartfelt, and authentic manner. Sorting and clarifying things and reclaiming connection with your loved one become more important to you than proving that you are right and he is wrong

- Practice universal love.

Increase the width of your love by including more people. When you practice universal love and caring, you improve your well-being, as well as those of people around you.

Application: A Brief Mindfulness Meditation to Open Your Heart and Cultivate Compassion

Sit down. Close your eyes. Breathe deeply.

Imagine that you are surrounded by the people you value deeply in your life. You are in the center of this loving circle. Imagine every person in the group sending you warm, loving thoughts -- "May you find joy in your life." "May you be safe and healthy." "May you find peace and calm in your heart."

Start sending the same loving messages to yourself.

Be open to the love. It is given freely, without condition. You don't have to do anything to deserve it. You exist – that is all the reason you need.

Open your heart and spirit to receive all these warm, loving thoughts.

Imagine yourself feeling warm with the joy that comes from being on the receiving end of all these messages of care, attention, regard, and energy. Focus on how you feel as you open yourself to receive this outpouring of love. Imagine warm, loving energy as it seeps through your skin and into your very being. Bask in the energizing love and feel the rejuvenation that comes from it.

Imagine the love coming your way energize and transform you into someone eager to give that love back. Send the same loving thoughts to the people around you. Let the same love, care, compassion, and energy that come from the people in the circle flow right back to them. Then imagine yourself sending the same loving thoughts to the universe.

"May all of us be safe and healthy."

"May all of us be protected."

"May all of us find joy in our lives."

"May all of us find peace."

"May all of us be blessed."

"May all of us find peace and calm in our hearts."

Chapter 4: Mindfulness and Self-Esteem: Keep in Mind that You Are Good Enough!

"At the center of your being you have the answer; you know who you are and you know what you want." – Lao Tzu

A person with low self-esteem feels inadequate. He often feels inept, awkward, and unlovable. Because of his fragile and weak sense of self, he is often hypersensitive and easily hurt by other people.

A person with low self-esteem often feels rebuffed and rejected, even for no justifiable reason. He thinks that other people disapprove of him or think badly of him. He sees rejection even where none exists. As a consequence, he sees himself as not good enough. He lacks the self-confidence to assert himself – in school, at work, or in his relationships.

Other people may criticize you. They may openly ridicule you or put you down. They may point out your flaws to you. These actions are likely to challenge your self-esteem.

Studies show, however, that self-esteem is usually most vulnerable, not to what other people say about you, but to how you think of yourself. Your inner critic who passes judgment on you may be a greater threat to your self-esteem than how other people look at you. You become your most severe (and most hurtful) critic when you pass judgment on how you feel and what you think and do.

When you make an error in judgment, do you rebuke yourself without compassion? When your memory fails you, do you chide yourself? When you find yourself acting childishly, making mistakes, breaking your promises, or failing in your relationships, do you censure yourself and find it difficult to forgive yourself?

You can do a wide range of things that you may eventually regret. Everybody does. The important thing is to forgive yourself, rise up, and give yourself a second chance – and even a third, or fourth, or even a fifth chance. Stop harshly criticizing yourself. It can only result in a negative self-image which, in turn, leads to bigger emotional problems.

Constantly berate yourself for not being "good with people" and you may eventually find yourself avoiding all interactions – or you may become defensive, cynical, and act horribly when you are with other people.

When you label yourself as unlovable, awkward, shy, loathsome, incompetent, etc, you will find it difficult to believe that other people see you otherwise. You think that they see you in the same manner. As a result, you become very unhappy.

Building Self-Esteem

The good news is that you CAN build self-esteem. You can turn your negative self-image around and build healthy self-appreciation and confidence. You can achieve a healthy sense of self.

Here are some mindful ways to increase self-esteem and confidence.

• Be mindfully aware about how your inner critic is working against you.

What does the critical voice inside your head constantly tell you?

"I am stupid."

"I am fat and ugly."

"Nobody likes me."

"I always make a fool of myself."

"I am a no-good person."

"I always fail."

"I am worthless."

If you want to grow in self-esteem, you need to become aware of these nagging thoughts, challenge them, and replace them with positive affirmations. You need to stand up to the voice in your head that tells you that you are not good enough.

Challenge your inner critic by cultivating a more positive, realistic, and loving appraisal of yourself.

"I am stupid." Challenge this by thinking, "I may have made some mistakes but I am efficient, competent, and smart in a lot of ways."

Look mindfully into what is good about you and use these strengths to challenge your inner critic.

- Treat yourself like a friend.

Treat yourself as you would treat a good friend. You have compassion for a friend you love. You treat him with kindness. You take him for what he is. You do not stand in judgment of him. Act towards yourself in like manner.

- Don't compare yourself with others.

Some people always measure themselves against others. This is a mistake. There will always be people much better than you are just as there will always be people who will be less fortunate than you are.

Do not allow your self-esteem to depend on other people's perceptions, your outward accomplishments, or how you compare with others. When you do, your self-esteem is likely to rise and fall depending on your most recent achievements or failures.

Think instead about the kind of person you want to grow into. See to it that the goals you set and the actions you take align with your values.

• Earn self-respect.

You tend to hold yourself in high esteem if you know that you are living according to your values and moral code.

If a healthy lifestyle is important to you, refrain from smoking or using drugs. These actions will create dissonant feelings within yourself and arouse your inner critic into assailing your self-esteem.

• Look for something meaningful to do.

As a human being, you feel good when you do something meaningful, help other people, or take part in advocacies that are bigger than yourself. Contributing to efforts to make a better society is a beautiful and productive way to build confidence and grow in self-esteem.

• Don't regard mistakes as "bad."

Don't brush off mistakes or failures as character flaws. Look at them as opportunities to learn, collect helpful insights, address a problem area, and grow.

• Use visualization.

Create a clear image of the self you want to become. Visualize this image as often as you can.

Studies show that when you play a positive version of yourself in your mind over and over again, you help the image become a reality. You tap the subconscious to identify resources (both internal and external) and activate them. You trigger the law of attraction and set opportunities in motion. You motivate yourself to do what is necessary to become what you want to be.

Mindful visualization of your "best" self helps you overcome the poor (and often inaccurate) self-image responsible for the loss of self-confidence.

• Always recognize and celebrate the times when you are doing well.

People with poor self-esteem usually focus on mistakes and on what is going wrong in their lives. Do the opposite and focus on what is going well. What are you doing right?

This attitude is a game changer. It sets the right tone for the day. It makes you look forward to getting more things right.

• Boot out negative thoughts.

Tied up to the tip above, safeguard your mind and spirit from unhealthy and negative thoughts. Be vigilant. Negativity usually leads to an insecure mindset and disposition.

• Explore your inner world.

"Hmmm, I reacted quite interestingly when I did that. I wonder if it was because of something I am scared of or something I am trying to avoid."

"Hmmm, I wonder how I would feel if I try not to control how situations turn out. Will I feel calmer?"

Practice reflecting on what goes on within you. When you know how your thoughts trigger emotions and behaviors, you set the stage for overcoming your insecurities.

- Take risks.

You will never know if you will succeed unless you go for it. As you grow older, your life becomes narrower. Taking risks now helps to save you from having bitter regrets later.

- Act as if you already were.

If you want self-confidence, act as if you ARE self-confident. Behave as if you already have what you want.

Assuming a power pose (standing up tall and straight, chin held high, shoulders rolled back, arms in an open, confident position) will eventually make you feel strong and confident even if you weren't at the start. If the confidence does not come soon enough, you will at least get some people to think that you are, indeed, self confident if they go by your body language!

Take action even if you feel you would fail. If things succeed, you will realize that you are REALLY self-confident! If things don't go as expected, mine the situation for insights. Either way, you are in a better place compared to where you would be if you refuse to take any action at all.

- Be your own cheerleader.

Don't wait for others to give you the affirmation that you need. Be your own cheerleader.

Take stock of your strengths. Think of as many as you can. Don't be shy about it. Don't be inhibited. Believe in yourself.

- Take time off.

The journey towards becoming your best self will not be smooth all the way. When you hit some rough spots, give yourself time out to boost your moods.

Give yourself some form of treat. It doesn't have to be something impressive. Your favorite upbeat song, a massage, a frolic session with your pet, a professional manicure or anything that makes you feel good will do the trick.

- Get out of your comfort zone once in a while.

Are you afraid to speak to a large crowd? Take small strides outside your comfort zone and build your self-confidence little by little.

Start a podcast. Give a speech in front of a small group of family and friends. Give a lecture. After taking a step, give yourself a pat on the back. Reward yourself with a small treat.

- Release stress.

Self-esteem starts to waver when the going gets difficult. Fear, stress, uncertainty, and feeling overwhelmed often crush confidence. Use mindfulness to maintain clarity, focus, and serenity.

Go for a mindful jog around your home. Meditate. Do mindful yoga. Have a cup of tea.

- Re-think your idea of confidence.

Some people hesitate to develop confidence, afraid that others may see them as arrogant, proud, or haughty.

People with arrogance and pride are usually judgmental and condescending. They intimidate others. They make others lose confidence and feel insecure, uncertain, and even inferior.

True self-confidence is based on a strong acceptance of self (limitations, as well as strengths). It implies openness to growth and feedback. A person with this disposition is likely to have the same open and accepting disposition towards other people.

Self-confidence inspires others. It builds morale. It makes other people feel confident, too.

- Keep something that reminds or inspires you to be confident.

A token of confidence can be anything – a necklace, rosary, perfume, a special set of earrings, or a new dress.

When you associate self-confidence with this particular token, it reminds you to breathe, practice positive affirmation, and focus on the here and now to feel supported, loved, and grounded.

- Be kind and compassionate.

Show simple acts of kindness. Smile, buy an ice-cream for a sad friend, call your mom to see how she is, or listen to someone with an open and encouraging attitude.

Being kind makes you feel good. And when you feel good inside, you radiate confidence.

Chapter 5: Focus! Focus! Focus!

"Don't dissipate your powers; strive to concentrate them." – Goethe

The ability to focus and direct your mental energy toward something specific is essential to learning, high-quality performance, and the achievement of goals. Studies demonstrate that people who are able to sustain their attention for a longer period of time perform better on challenges compared to those who have poor concentration. Mental focus can be the critical factor in doing well, whether it is being able to finish a marathon or a difficult report at work.

It is difficult to stay on task. Staying focused becomes particularly difficult when you have to contend with constant distractions.

Fortunately, focus CAN be developed. The mind is like a muscle that you can work out and strengthen.

Just as you can strengthen your body, you can also strengthen your mind. You can build its power and stamina by giving it purposeful exercise, as well as the time it needs to rest, be still, and recover.

Mindful Strategies for Sharpening Focus and Attention

Here are some mindful strategies to help develop razor-sharp mental focus:

- Evaluate where you stand.

Before you start a program to build mental focus, it helps to know where you stand at the present moment. Just how strong or weak is your mental focus right now?

You have good mental focus if you have no issues with the following:

Staying alert and attentive

Setting your goals and breaking your tasks up into smaller and doable sections

Taking short breaks and then getting back to work

With just a little more practice, you will be able to hone the concentration skills you already have.

You need to work on your focus if you have the following problems:

You catch yourself daydreaming frequently.

You find it hard to tune out distractions.

You fail to monitor your progress.

It may take some time to develop laser-like focus. But with constant practice, you can form helpful habits to sustain focus and manage your distractibility better.

•　　　　Eliminate distractions.

One of the easier ways to sustain focus is to get rid or minimize the number of distractions which interfere with attention.

This is easier with some types of distractions. You can just turn off your phone or the television if they are your sources of distraction. How do you deal with a spouse, co-worker, roommate, or kids who often interrupt your attention when you are working?

You have several options. You can opt to work undisturbed in another location that is more quiet and private – a private room designated as "office" in your home, the local library, or your favorite coffee shop. You can also designate certain hours of the day as "don't disturb" hours.

Distractions can also come from within in the form of anxiety, fatigue, or poor motivation. Minimize these distractions by getting adequate rest before your task or using mindful imagery and positive thoughts to reduce worrying thoughts. Every time your mind starts to wander because of distracting thoughts, intentionally bring your attention back to what you are doing.

•　　　　Avoid multi-tasking.

Some people find multi-tasking an amazing way to do a number of tasks quickly. Most people, however, are not good at multi-tasking.

Multi-tasking can be counter-productive. It ruins focus. It makes it difficult to hone in on the finer details of a task.

Focus your attention on one task and you see things clearly. Spread it over multiple tasks, and you run the risk of failing to notice some important details.

• Focus on the moment.

Keep thinking about the past. Worry about the future. Tune out from the task at hand. All these keep you from being present. They prevent you from being completely engaged in the here and now (the task at hand).

Being fully present sharpens your mental focus. It keeps your attention razor-sharp. It enables your mental resources to hone in on what really matters at this particular point in time.

• Take short breaks.

When you do something for a long period of time, your focus tends to wear off. You will find it harder to apply all your mental resources to what you are doing. You will also become less efficient.

Take breaks. When you shift your attention on to something unrelated even for a short while, your mental focus improves dramatically.

When you sit down to do something that requires more time (study for an exam or do your taxes, for example), take an occasional break. Even a short moment of respite serves to energize you and sharpen mental clarity and focus. It enables you to keep your performance at peak levels.

• Practice mindfulness meditation.

Studies show that people who meditate are able to focus longer, let their attention wander less frequently, and find less need to repeatedly switch tasks. They are able to work more efficiently.

Most people associate meditation with keeping cool and calm. While meditation can, indeed, help generate serenity, studies show that it is also helpful for enhancing focus and concentration.

You don't have to go to a monastery or high up in the mountains to meditate. You don't even have to meditate for a long period of time to enjoy the benefits. All you need is just 10-20 minutes of daily meditation for you to reap the rewards.

Kick start your mornings by meditating. Do deep breathing and stay with the breath for just a few minutes. You will see a change in your mental clarity and focus within a few days.

- Use deep breathing to quickly regain focus.

Intrusive thoughts keep you from being fully engaged in the task at hand. Regain focus by taking time off to do deep breathing.

Focus on your breath. Take deep breaths and stay tuned in on each breath. When your attention wanders from it, gently nudge it back.

Do the exercise anytime and anywhere, especially when you can't concentrate. In time, you will find it easier to keep your attention where it belongs.

- Incorporate short mindfulness sessions in your daily schedule.

Look for opportunities to practice mindfulness every day.

Just slow down, focus on what you are doing, and be aware of all the physical sensations, thoughts, and emotions that you are going through at that particular moment.

When you eat, slow down to chew the food and experience its colors, texture, and taste. When you shave, enjoy the scent of your shaving cream, luxuriate in the feel of the warm lather against your skin, and slowly draw the razor over the dark stubble.

Being mindful in simple ways every day teaches you to focus and to manage distractions. It teaches you to be here now. Mindfulness (being in the moment and being fully aware of your breath and sensations) strengthens and expands your attention span. It prepares you to focus and fight the restless itch that nags you to stop working and do something else.

• Continue to practice.

You can't sharpen mental focus overnight. You need time and practice to strengthen focus and hone concentration.

Once you recognize the negative effects that come with constantly being sidetracked from doing what really matters in your life, start to build your mental focus.

Regular practice will help you make the most favorable use of your time. It will help you use time to focus on the things that bring meaning, satisfaction, and joy to your life.

Application: Mindfully Increasing Focus

If you know that your ability to focus at present is at ground zero, choose to build it up gradually.

A person who wants to train for the first time in order to get in shape physically should do so slowly. If he throws himself into an intense training program right away, he will end up discouraged or injured, or both. Chances are he will quit before he has really even started.

The same works for building mental focus.

For example, you work online as a writer. You are easily distracted. You find it difficult to sit on your desk and write for even 10 minutes straight.

Set a goal that you know you can manage pretty well and use that as your base line.

Require yourself to work/research/write for 5 minutes. Focus on the task just for the 5 minutes. Set the timer and when it goes off, take a break for 2 minutes.

After this short break, do focused work again for another 5 minutes. Follow this up with another short break.

Every day, put in an additional 5 minutes to work with focus. Increase your break time likewise with an extra 2 minutes. On your 9th day, you will be working for 45 minutes straight followed by an 18-minute break.

Give yourself time to feel completely comfortable with this system. You can then add more focused work time and shorten your break times if you feel the need for it.

Support your efforts to focus by making a distraction to-do list. This list is going to be particularly useful if you are working online.

When you have a problem with attention span, you will find that a good number of things (not related to the task at hand) tend to cross your mind from time to time.

"Will it snow tomorrow? I wonder what the weather forecast is."

"I wonder if I can find a good recipe for the lasagna I want to prepare for dinner tonight."

Before you know it, you are interrupting the flow of what you are doing to Google the information. Studies show that when you allow yourself to be distracted from a task, you need about 25 minutes to regain your focus and get back to the task at hand. Moreover, having to shift your focus back and forth weakens concentration, and depletes its intensity and strength.

To stay on track, make a distraction to-do list, Every time something unrelated to the task at hand pops into your mind, jot it down. Tell yourself that you will look it up when you stop your focused work for your break.

By doing this, you are able to intentionally shelve distractions for a later time, and use the time allotted for work purposefully to concentrate on the task at hand.

Chapter 6: Apply Mindfulness in Daily Routines

"The little things? The little moments? They aren't little." - **Jon Kabat-Zinn**

There has been a relatively recent surge of interest in mindfulness. This increase in public awareness about mindfulness, in turn, has given rise to new academic literature and studies about the concept. Google "mindfulness" and you will find a great number of empirical studies about the construct.

Because of the growing "clinical" interest and approach to mindfulness, as well as its association with Buddhist contemplation practices, some people tend to view mindfulness as something that is "sophisticated" or "complicated."

Mindfulness is anything but complicated.

It simply means being in the moment, being present, being aware and open to the here and now.

Every moment in your everyday life gives you the opportunity to apply mindfulness and enjoy its rewards. All you have to do is to find a way to be mindful, a way that works favorably for you and your lifestyle. You can be mindful for 15 seconds, or for 15 minutes, or for a couple of hours each day. Every single time that you practice mindfulness adds up; each moment helps you live your life more fully, in the here and now.

How do you integrate mindfulness into your daily life? Here are some ways to do so:

• Set the tone for your day by practicing mindfulness in the morning.

Don't bolt out of bed when you wake up. Instead, use the first moments of each day to slowly stretch and be mindful. It is a gentle and beautiful way to start the day.

When you take the time sit down, to be still, and to do your mindfulness practice shortly after you wake, you condition your nervous system to seek little mindful moments during the day.

You also set the tone for your day. You condition your mind and heart to be serene, calm, and joyful.

Instead of checking your phone or email or listening to the news, have your "sit" and start your day in the right frame of mind.

• Bring the "monkey mind" lovingly and without judgment back to the present.

Sometimes, it may seem like your mind is in constant motion. It seems to jump around non-stop, moving from one worrying, unhappy thought to another and making you anxious, restless, unhappy, or angry.

These negative thoughts may include any of the following:

- worries about the many things that you have to do

- fears, either real or imaginary

- past experiences that have caused you pain and hurt

- non-stop judgments about the present

- "what-if" scenarios

Zen Buddhists use the term "monkey mind" to refer to this uninterrupted prattle that goes on in the mind.

Monkey mind makes you unable to concentrate. It is stressful. It makes it difficult to slow down and take in the present.

Practicing mindfulness in daily life helps to tame the monkey mind. It clears the mind. It enables you to focus on the task at hand. It gives you a sense of wellbeing and calm. It makes you a more peaceful and happier person.

- Keep it short.

The brain responds better to short stretches of mindfulness. It is better to do a few minutes of mindfulness spread out throughout the day than a weekend retreat or even one long drawn-out session.

Tuning in to your body for 10 minutes while you do your yoga in the morning and another 10 minutes while you go on a short walk in the afternoon can do a lot to clear and refresh your mind.

• Use your waiting time mindfully.

In today's fast-paced life, you have so many things to do that it can get quite frustrating to be stuck in traffic or to wait in line. Waiting can seem like a big waste of time.

Instead of looking at having to wait as a nuisance, see it as an opportunity. Use it to focus your mind on your breath and how it slowly flows in and out of your body. Become aware of the present, even of your frustration or impatience, without judging, allowing everything to simply be.

• Slow down.

More often than not, your typical day overflows with thoughts about things you have to do, deadlines to meet, and goals to strive for and achieve.

Does this state of affairs make you happy? Or do you sometimes feel shortchanged to live a life like this?

Instill a sense of calm, order, and serenity into your life by slowing down. Each moment that you are present in will seem more precious. You will get more joy and satisfaction from it.

Take time off from your busy work schedule, and take your family to a picnic in the park. Take your shoes off and feel the sensation of the grass under your feet. Look up at the sky and drink in the colors and the patterns that the clouds make. Look at trees around you and feel the breeze as it slowly flutters through the leaves.

When you slow down, you see the beauty that is present in the ordinary.

- Use your senses.

Mindfulness allows you to break free from the noisy, uninterrupted chatter of the mind, and get in touch with the stillness that lies within you. It allows you to let go of your compulsive thoughts and be aware of what is present.

Find your way into this state by using your senses. Explore the "here and now" with bare awareness – without judgment.

Your senses keep you in touch with the world. However, when you remain caught up in your thoughts, you fail to be truly present in the here and now. You are lost in either your fears or your daydreams, and fail to appreciate the present.

Use your senses intentionally and you become truly present in what is before you.

When you take a break from work and go for a short walk, feel the warmth of the sun against your skin and the breeze as it ruffles your hair. Be present to the sounds – be it the traffic noise or the chirping of the birds. Take a deep breath and be present to the scents you inhale.

When you use your senses to become fully engaged in the present, you cut short the mental noise. You bring a sense of aliveness into your day.

Application: Mindfulness in Simple Everyday Activities

There are things that you do day in and day out as part of your daily grind. You become so accustomed to doing them that you do them on auto-pilot mode. You go through the motions without even thinking much about them.

As a result, your mind fills with thoughts unrelated to what you are doing. You are doing one thing and thinking of another thing (or things). You worry. You fret. You daydream. Because of these distractions, you become disengaged from the present.

There are many opportunities during an ordinary day to practice mindfulness.

: Breakfast

Breakfast presents a wonderful chance to connect with your senses. Use this time to have a mindful moment.

Focus on the aroma of the coffee beans as your coffee brews. Feel the warmth of the coffee as you pour it into your cup.

Take a sip of the freshly brewed coffee and be present to how it smells and tastes. Does it taste nutty and earthy? Does it have fruity or floral undertones? Does it have caramel or chocolate accents? Take note of the mouth fill as you drink. Is it full, medium, or light? How about the aftertaste? Is it crisp or sharp?

Take a close look at your piece of toast. Become fully aware of its beautiful golden-brown color. See how the sides are crusty and how the center retains a little "give." See how the butter slowly melts as you smear it on the hot bread.

Notice how the hot toast feels in your hand. Observe the crumb trail the toast leaves on your plate. Take a small bite and savor the crunch and the slightly nutty taste as you bite into your toast. Chew slowly. Pay attention to the smell, taste, and texture.

: Washing the dishes

Practice mindfulness when you are doing your daily household chores. Sweeping the floor, washing the dishes, and folding the laundry – all these present amazing opportunities to practice a moment of mindfulness.

When you are washing the dishes, notice how the warm, soapy water feels against your hands. Be aware of the texture of the spoons, forks, and plates as you wash them. Be mindful of the motions you go though as you soap, scrub, and rinse everything, taking note of your need to see to it that everything comes out sparkling clean.

As you stay in front of the sink, notice your thoughts move to what is happening around you. Acknowledge these thoughts without allowing their storylines to preoccupy you. Gently veer your focus back to what you are doing.

Notice how your arms and hands move as you wash the dishes. If you feel a slight ache after a while, recognize the feeling. Be mindful about the sense of satisfaction you feel when you finish the chore.

: Bedtime

As the day ends, your body and mind tend to naturally wind down from all the activity and stress. They start to slow down and prepare for rest. Center your mindfulness practice during this time to intentionally unwind, do less, and relax in preparation for restful sleep.

Move mindfully through the motions to prepare for bed.

Take a soothing soak in the bath and feel the tension leave both your mind and body. Brush your teeth while taking note of the cool minty smell and taste of the toothpaste, and the feel of the toothbrush against your teeth. Be present to how your hand moves as it directs the toothbrush alongside your teeth. Focus on how clean and fresh your mouth feels after you brush your teeth.

Lie down comfortably on your bed and carry out a body scan.

Focus on one part of the body first.

Focus on your right foot. Is it cold or hot? Is it uncomfortable, tense, or relaxed? Just observe. Be present to how the foot feels without any judgment. Intentionally tense the muscles in your foot. Release the tension and relax the foot.

Transfer your focus to your right thigh, knee, and calf. Carry out the same motions -- scan, tense the muscles, and then let go of the tension.

Do the same thing with the left leg.

Transfer your focus to the right hand and arm, and then to the left hand and arm, doing the same thing you did with the foot. Repeat the exercise with the other parts of the body – stomach, chest, back, shoulders, and face.

If you find your mind wandering during the body scan, recognize the thoughts in a non-judgmental way, and then bring your focus gently back to the body scan.

The body scan exercise in mindfulness helps to relax both body and mind and promote sound sleep.

Chapter 7: Keep a Journal to Grow Deeper in Mindfulness

"Journaling is like whispering to one's self and listening at the same time." - Mina Murray

"Fill your paper with the breathings of your heart." William Wordsworth

Putting your thoughts down in paper can provide more benefits than most people realize. It is a powerful, effective and yet easy way to slow down, calm your spirit, get in touch with your inner self, and go deeper into your mindfulness practice.

Depending on what you put down on your journal, journaling can be a useful tool to help you do any (or all) of the following:

- Set your goals

- Plan your day or week

- Practice gratitude

- Listen to what your heart says

- Be conscious of your thought patterns

- Connect with your body

- Appreciate your surroundings

- Deepen self-understanding

- Understand and appreciate your relationships

- Let go

Mindfulness in its purest form is being in the present (in the now). However, it goes beyond just being cognizant of what is happening now. It includes understanding the why, where, who, and how of the present. It includes context. It includes understanding how the present came to be. It includes being aware of where you are at present and knowing how the now came to be.

Mindfulness is an art. Fortunately, it is an art that anyone can learn and cultivate, and journaling is one of the more effective tools for going deeper into the mindfulness practice.

Journaling promotes the practice of presence. It helps you get in touch with your thoughts and feelings. It deepens your awareness (and appreciation) of your surroundings and relationships. It inspires insight. It empowers your decisions and choices.

Journaling helps to make any given memory tangible. It encourages you to be more observant about everything that is in the experience, including your thoughts, feelings, surroundings, and people you interact with. When you put down the fine details of the memory on your journal, the memory becomes real again. You are able to reflect and contemplate on the experience, deepening your awareness once again.

When you spend time to write about any memory – be it nostalgic, stressful, joyful, worrisome, exciting, irritating, discouraging, or heartening, you are taking the time here and now, to pause and contemplate on these feelings. Journaling keeps you connected to the present, while allowing you to take a step back from the feelings that grip you. It gives you the chance to look at the experience – and yourself, from a distance.

When you go through an experience that causes you a great deal of anxiety or worry, you tend to lose yourself in the chaos that surrounds that emotion. When you write about that same experience, articulating that you are anxious or worried, you go through something that is one step removed. You develop a greater awareness about what you are going through. You are able to break it down, look at it, and consider your options.

You may not always find a solution; however, the mere act of writing helps you to ease the intensity of your emotions. You give your feelings gentle attention and space. As a result, the turmoil associated with the feelings subsides. It weakens its hold on you.

Journaling brings about results similar to those of meditation. In fact, many people call it meditative writing. It gives you the chance to get in touch with your inner self and reflect about what lies within. It makes you see what you really think and feel. By getting your thoughts from your head and into your journal, you become truly present.

By making you draw on your memory and articulate it, journaling allows you to focus on the experience and absorb it. It enables you to give time and space for your thoughts and feelings. It opens the door for you to put down on paper your doubts, fears, and resentments and, by so doing, move past them. It encourages you to look at yourself without judgment, to show yourself love, and to heal.

Application: Making Journaling a Part of Your Mindfulness Practice

If you are a beginner at journaling, start with just 10 minutes to sit down and write on your journal. Write for yourself. Be open and honest.

Let journaling become a habit. Let it be an intrinsic part of your daily practice of being mindful. It will help you become more aware, more reflective, and more insightful. It will help you grow in understanding and wisdom.

There are different ways to use a journal to help you make progress in your mindfulness journey. Go over these suggestions from people who swear on the great benefits that come from sustaining the journaling habit. Apply those that resonate with you.

- Use it as a planning tool to make you feel less overwhelmed.

Look to the week ahead. Use your journal to schedule your personal commitments, work, and social obligations. Include things that give you joy and pleasure like recipes that you want to try out, time for exercise, time for yoga or meditation, and other similar interests.

- Look for something that makes you feel grateful.

When you are struggling with something in your life, this may seem difficult to do; nevertheless, just do it. That "something" does not have to be grand. It can be something simple like the satisfying creamy taste and mouth feel of a dollop of cream added to your morning cup of coffee. It can be a favorite melody playing on the radio.

If you make a practice of being grateful, you will soon realize that this simple habit helps to sustain you in times of great challenge or heartbreak. It gives you hope. It helps you recognize and celebrate even the little joys that give color and meaning to your life.

- Use journaling to help achieve your goals.

This may sound a bit fanciful. How does the simple act of scribbling about your dreams help you achieve them?

You can't build a house without a blueprint, can you? When you put your dreams and goals down in writing, you send your brain the message that "these dreams are important to me." Your subconscious then flags pertinent information and opportunities to help make your dreams come true.

-   Use it to build self-discipline.

When you set aside time to write on your journal, you are instilling self-discipline. You are forming a good habit – and a good habit tends to make it easier to form other good habits.

•   Use it to reduce stress.

Stress is often a result of having your emotions blocked or of getting caught up in terrifying "what-ifs."

Journaling gives you the means to translate a difficult emotional experience or an apprehension about the future into words. By so doing, you become better able to grasp and face your trauma or fear. You untangle yourself from it and set yourself free. It is not surprising that health care experts recommend expressive writing as one of the more effective routes to heal from physical, psychological, and emotional pains.

•   Use journaling to invite the feelings you'd like to have into your heart.

For instance, on a day that you feel particularly sad or exhausted, write affirmations like "I am energized." "I am full of hope and life." "I look forward to what this day holds for me." When you feel nervous about a presentation you are scheduled to make for that day, write something like "I am confident." "I am going to slay this." Pretty soon, you will find yourself actually feeling positive about your day and what it holds for you.

- Use it to write from the heart.

Tell everything as it is in your journal.

Do not disguise the bad parts. Include the difficult bits. When you let yourself face even the things that give you pain, you begin to develop courage and compassion. You help yourself grow.

Write your thoughts as they are – dark, ugly, beautiful, or uplifting. When you put them in writing and see them in black and white, you will learn who you truly are; you may even get fresh insights about where you need to go.

Write freely, without censure or judgment. Consider your journal as a safe place, a place where you can acknowledge and embrace all that you are, both good and bad.

When you go over your journal a few weeks hence and read the emotions you have articulated, you will find yourself feeling more kindly and more compassionate towards yourself.

- Use it to foster respect and love.

When going through a heated discussion with someone you love, step back a bit. Resolve to listen actively, to get some insights about how the other person thinks and feels, as well as why he feels or thinks this way. Try to get context.

Writing about the experience will give you the opportunity to reflect on the discussion. It will help you generate fresh insights and to deepen your understanding. Going over the transcript of your conversation will help promote better understanding, acceptance, respect, and love.

- Use it to foster a healthy and mindful regard for your physical, mental, and emotional health.

Ascertain where your health stands right now. Write down how you plan to pull through, improve, or rejuvenate.

Follow your progress with regular journal entries. Celebrate the advancements in your health and well-being. Reflect on what you can do to make things better.

Revisit your journal the next time you feel that something is off-kilter. Chances are high that you will find something in your entries to help you recover.

Chapter 8: Teach Your Kids How to Be Mindful

"Yesterday's the past, tomorrow's the future, but today is a gift. That's why it's called the present." – Bil Keane

Mindfulness is beneficial not just for adults. It can also be of great advantage to your children.

An increasing number of studies show that mindfulness can help kids to be more attentive, sustain interest and focus, and make better decisions. Mindfulness also helps kids regulate their emotions. It helps ease tension and reduce stress. It helps kids view themselves and other people with more understanding and compassion.

Even kids go through tough times. They get hungry, irritable, and tired. They get upset, hurt, and angry. They find it difficult to control their emotions. They don't know how to communicate what they feel and may burst out in fits of temper.

As teenagers, they go through an even more difficult and awkward stage and deal with even more complicated problems. They have to navigate through puberty, hormonal changes, school pressures, peer pressure, relationships, the need to exercise independence, and so on. These struggles, both external and internal, can feel quite overwhelming.

Growing up is not easy.

One way you can help your kids deal with life is to teach them mindfulness.

Being able to pay attention to the here and now, with an open, accepting, and non-judgmental disposition, can be a very powerful and useful tool to help your kids steer their way through life.

Mindfulness continues to take its place among other practices as a popular mainstream practice for living life with more grace, purpose, and joy. It is helping not only corporate executives, athletes, parents and other adults but kids as well.

Teach your kids to embrace the mindfulness practice now and you empower them with the habit of living a life of peace, serenity, acceptance, and kindness. You teach them how to reduce stress and live more joyfully. You give them the strength and ability to face whatever problems life has in store for them. You give them the gift of finding beauty and joy in the here and now.

Strategies for Teaching Your Kids the Mindfulness Habit

Keep the following in mind when teaching mindfulness to your kids:

- Model the habit.

The most effective way to teach mindfulness to your kids is to practice it yourself. When your kids see you making the effort to be in the present – and see how the practice is helping you become a better person, they will be more likely to try to be like you.

- Check your expectations.

One of the core principles of the mindfulness habit is to let go of expectations, to be nonjudgmental.

Why do you want to teach mindfulness to your kids? Is it because you want a quiet home? Is it because you want to do away with tantrums?

Kids whine. They argue, fight, and get into tantrums. They are noisy and exuberant; they often get underfoot. This is the way they are NATURALLY. Mindfulness is not a panacea. You can't expect your kids to stop acting like normal kids by teaching them mindfulness.

What mindfulness does is to give your kids direction so they become more aware of their experiences (from both an outer and inner point of view), see their fears and apprehensions as "just thoughts," and be able to reduce anxiety.

Mindfulness teaches them to focus and concentrate, as well as to recognize when their attention wanders and how to bring it back to the task at hand. It teaches them to recognize the emotions that they are going through, and how to view them without judgment. It teaches them to breathe, take time off, and not react impulsively. It teaches them how to nurture compassion, for themselves as well as for other people.

- Keep things simple.

Kids are not likely to appreciate big words. Present mindfulness to your kids as simply being aware or noticing – noticing their thoughts, what the body feels, what they hear, see, smell, touch, taste, and the things that are happening at present or going on around them right here, right now.

- Introduce a mindful ritual at bedtime.

Kids love rituals. Teach them how to do a short body scan meditation when they turn in for sleep. Ask them to close their eyes, and bring their attention to their feet, legs, belly, back, chest, shoulders, and face.

The body scan meditation is a calming and fun way to teach them to return to their body before going to sleep.

- Assign a breathing buddy.

When you tell your kids to "focus on or follow your breath," they may not understand what you mean.

Make the exercise easier for your kids by assigning a favorite stuffed toy as their breathing buddy. Ask your kids to lie down and put the toy on their belly. Ask them to focus on the toy as it rises and falls as they breathe in and out.

- Take "noticing walks."

Make things fun. Take your kids on a stroll around your neighborhood and tell them that you are taking a "noticing walk."

Tell them that you will take a couple of minutes to stay absolutely quiet and simply listen to everything that they hear – a lawnmower at use, birds chirping, frogs croaking, a dog barking, etc.

On another day, ask them to go for another walk and to pay attention to what they see in detail – the patterns that the clouds make on the sky, the blades of grass moving with the breeze, the play of sun and shadow on the ground, and so on and so forth.

You don't even have to label the walks as mindful walks – but that is exactly what they are.

- Nurture an attitude of gratitude.

Teach your kids to be grateful.

The ability to look at life with a grateful heart is an essential component of being mindful. It involves looking at life from the vantage point of appreciating what is there, instead of focusing on what is not there.

You can't teach gratitude by nagging your kids into learning the value. You have to live it.

Look for opportunities to model gratitude.

Say "thank you" often and sincerely. It indicates that you appreciate every blessing that comes your way. You don't feel entitled to any of them.

Teach them to be compassionate to those who are less fortunate. Encourage them to help grandma, a neighbor, or a classmate who is in a tight spot. This helps them recognize their blessings and nurture the willingness to share them with others.

Teach them to recognize even simple moments in their day that inspire awe – an amazingly gorgeous sunset, the heart-warming sound of a baby's laughter, a cool drink after play -- and express their joy and gratitude for these moments.

Establish a gratitude ritual at dinner. Going around the table, ask each member of the family to verbalize his gratitude. Another option is to ask your kids to share with you what special things the day had for them before you tuck them in to sleep.

Compliment others. This will encourage your kids to recognize and acknowledge the things they like about another person.

Encourage them to have a gratitude journal where they can express their gratitude in ways that work for them – in writing, painting, or drawing. Or you may want your family to have a family gratitude journal which everybody can access and use to share their stories.

Encourage them to look for the positive even in difficult or frustrating situations. Help them to work through feelings of resentment or envy. Show them that these feelings are often a result of focusing on what other people have, instead of feeling grateful for the many blessings in their own lives.

- Help your kids to get in touch with their feelings.

Help them identify their feelings by using the terms usually used in weather reports – calm, sunny, rainy, windy, stormy, tsunami, etc. "I feel that it is raining but it has not really turned into a storm."

Using terms that they are familiar with helps them become aware of their feelings without identifying with them too much. It brings home the realization that just as you can't change the weather, they can't change how they feel either. What they CAN change is how they view or relate to these feelings.

- Always be on the lookout for "teachable" moments.

It is good to have regular conversations about the values that you want your kids to learn. However, there is nothing like a real-life situation to eloquently illustrate what you mean. Such a situation will make the lesson you are teaching come truly alive for your kids. It will make a strong impact on them and guarantee that your kids will understand, soak up, and remember what you are trying to teach them.

For instance, if you want to teach them how to be helpful, encourage them to do some errands for an elderly neighbor. Let them go through their things and choose clothes and toys that they can give to the less fortunate. Let them realize that it feels good to be able to help out.

• Don't force it.

When you are trying to teach your kids how to be mindful, and they don't seem receptive, leave it for the meantime. This is a good occasion for you to apply the mindful principle of showing no judgment and letting things be.

Application: Teaching Your Kids to Practice Mindful Eating

One of the easier and fun ways to teach kids how to slow down and be present is to teach them how to eat mindfully. The practice helps nurture awareness; it helps kids connect with the task at hand, as well as with what is going on inside them.

Walk through the following exercise with your kids so they will experience what it means to "eat mindfully."

Give each kid an orange. You may say something like the following:

> "We will now eat our orange in a mindful manner. This simply means that you pay attention to the orange – what it looks like, what it feels like, what it smells like, and what it tastes like.

> Take your time as you eat the orange. Do it slowly, without any rush, making sure that you observe everything there is about the orange, as well as your reactions to it.

> Hold the orange in your hand. Roll it around in your palm. What does the orange feel like in your hand?

> Take a long hard look at the orange. Feel it with your fingers. Is the skin of the orange bumpy? Smooth? When you hold it a bit more firmly, does the orange feel soft or squishy?

> Bring the orange close to your nose. Take a whiff. What scents do you notice? Does the orange smell sweet, sour, bitter, or citrusy?

Now start peeling the orange. How does the orange feel in your hand? Is the juice running out? Is the scent stronger?

Is your mouth starting to water? Get a small bite of the orange. Notice how the juice and flesh feel as you bite into the orange. Observe how it feels like against your tongue.

Take your time to chew the orange. Observe the texture, juiciness, tart-sweet taste of each bite. Savor each bite. Be present to it."

This simple exercise on mindful eating is a short and fun way for kids to learn how to slow down, focus, savor what they are eating and, by extension, simply be in the present and enjoy what it has to offer.

The End

Thanks for reading my book until the end.

I hope this book was able to deepen your understanding and appreciation of the mindfulness practice and how it contributes to a better life.

The next step is to apply the tips and techniques outlined for you so you can start applying the habits that will help you achieve a life free from stress and anxiety, a life that brims over with calmness, grace, and inner peace.

-   **Amy**